We Are gods!

GROUNDBREAKING INSIGHTS
FOR EVERY PARENT, TEACHER,
COACH, EMPLOYER, TEAM OR
ORGANIZATIONAL LEADER

Guy Massi

TRILOGY CHRISTIAN PUBLISHERS

TUSTIN, CA

Trilogy Christian Publishers

A Wholly Owned Subsidary of Trinity Broadcasting Network

2442 Michelle Drive

Tustin, CA 92780

For information, address Trilogy Christian Publishing

Rights Department, 2442 Michelle Drive, Tustin, Ca 92780.

Trilogy Christian Publishing/ TBN and colophon are trademarks of Trinity Broadcasting Network.

For information about special discounts for bulk purchases, please contact Trilogy Christian Publishing.

Manufactured in the United States of America

Trilogy Disclaimer: The views and content expressed in this book are those of the author and may not necessarily reflect the views and doctrine of Trilogy Christian Publishing or the Trinity Broadcasting Network.

10 9 8 7 6 5 4 3 2 1

Library of Congress Cataloging-in-Publication Data is available.

ISBN 978-1-64088-577-6

ISBN 978-1-64088-578-3

Contents

Plain and simple, I dedicate this book to God, His son Jesus Christ, the Holy Spirit who leads me, and my family; all of whom, if without, my talents and the manifestations thereof would not otherwise be possible.

Foreword

Serving as Lead Pastor of The Mission Church, I have known Guy Massi and his family for a dozen years. His wife is the director of our school and his children are beloved sons of our congregation. Guy is one of those brothers you can always count on. His love for people and commitment to community go "above and beyond." When he asked me to write the foreword of this book, I felt both honored and responsible to encourage and support his passion to put into words all that God has put into his heart.

I must admit, at first glance, I was a little uncomfortable with his use of the term "gods" (little "g"), as I'm sure some of his readers may also be. However, as Guy states in his introduction, "...there is only one true God, with a capital 'G'..." – the Creator of the heavens and earth and the redeemer of mankind, Jesus Christ. But his use of the term "gods" may give the reader the impression he believes in the existence of other, subservient deities.

Let me assure you, he does not.

Identifying the "gods" of this age is an important task. In life, we all have authority figures and influential role models that have been lifted up, in our minds, as key figures. Often the emphasis we place on them, the praise and deference we give to them, could cause us to overemphasize their power over us and in us; in essence, we can allow them to become our gods. Beyond that, many people, because of the elevated status they have in society in general and in people's lives in specific, they develop an overinflated view of themselves. Pride, egotism, and narcissism take over and they believe themselves more important than those over whom they have been elevated to serve. This is the classic dilemma of corruption. People who receive power, authority, and influence are corrupted by that influence and use it to benefit themselves rather than the ones they ought to be serving. It can be seen among politicians, business leaders, coaches, role models, and even parents.

When this happens, they become gods, albeit false gods.

Within this book, the reader will find helpful examples and practical instructions of leadership in its truest form: servanthood. I appreciate Guy's transparency beginning with the story of the loss of his father at a young age and later by navigating the challenges of life in young adulthood and beyond. His experiences present a helpful and inspirational backdrop for every person aspiring to achieve their potential and serve through leadership. Even more, aspiring leaders will discover safeguards, both internal and external, to prevent them from being pulled into the ubiquitous "god-complex" of our idol laden culture. It is that belief and expectation of feeling entitled to special privilege because of the special talents, abilities or positions they have received. Let us remember, as Guy points out, there is only one true God, the other "gods" of this age are false idols, made up in our minds.

Rev. Gregg T. Johnson
Lead Pastor, The Mission Church
Founder and President, Global Leadership Training

Preface

First, let me clarify one important inalienable fact. In my faith, there is only one true God, with a capital "G". He is the Creator of all things. He is not manufactured by man or one amongst many; He is the only God. He is the one I look to, and it is only by His grace that I am able to write this book. Really, this book has been in the works since I was eleven years old, during a time when I lost my primary male role model and lender – my father. I quickly learned that stand-in male role models (good or bad) could provide a template of masculinity which you may choose either to adopt or ignore. As I write this book, I am still not a master of all its principles, and I find that I have composed many of the pages out of sheer frustration and subsequent realizations. I am learning and evolving each day and I revisit my failures in an attempt to lead people away from life changing mistakes, while assisting others to embrace the words and encouragement of life's "gods" as well as the one true God in order to identify and follow the unique purpose for their lives. I actually "penned" this little book over the course of a very unique and challenging time of my life that elicited a forced growth in me, a growth necessary to almost every person. During the book's editing process, I often contemplated making drastic changes to the text to more accurately reflect the current state of myself. However, consideration revealed that in order for the essence of the messages contained herein to be appropriately delivered, they must be conveyed within the framework and context reflective of my state of emotional consciousness during that particular span of my life. In these chapters you will find that I often convey a stream of consciousness that becomes intertwined with both personal and organizational terminologies which become "interchangeable". (i.e. family, team, staff, colleagues, employees, coaches, etc.) Additionally and at times, I can become mildly abstract and veer towards my opinions concerning human psycho-environmental factors. (For both of these transgressions, I apologize in advance and ask for your patience.) As we take this journey, it will become evident to you (as it has to me) that anyone can potentially fall prey to developing a "god complex" in an attempt to assert control and become "gods" of our own daily habitats. How powerful, yet powerless we can be. I also wish to apologize to those that I have unknowingly or unduly offended in the course of life and continually attempt to recapture those things that are most important to me. I do appreciate one saying, however, that is relative to being a sensitive and productive "god"; don't mistake my kindness for weakness!

Acknowledgements

First and of course, I thank God! I thank Him for bringing me into relationship and understanding of what Jesus Christ should mean to me and to admit that I can do nothing through my own natural strength, but must remain completely reliant on the strength that I can only find in Him. (Life is just too tough to navigate without divine strength) I also owe a debt of gratitude to the following persons and for the following reasons: **my wife** – for always demonstrating compassion and providing the same example of love, understanding, and forgiveness on a daily basis; **all of my sons** – for allowing me to develop as a father and providing life lessons concerning the human spirit (Matt and Josh hugs are beyond compare); **Larry Capra** – my lifelong friend who is ever present to just listen to me during any type of "crisis"; **Pastor Gregg Johnson, Thomas Readyoff, Jerry Sauder, Terry Doyle and Gerard D'Ambrosio** for giving sacrificially of their own personal time and resources to provide me with sound counsel and support me during a potentially insurmountable set of challenges in my life; **Ronald Kaitz, Laurence Kolman and Jonathan Butters** for always challenging me to be a better husband and father and leading me to reflect upon my own accountability; **Craig Machado, Matt Cascioli and Konstantinos (Gus) Sofos** for always reminding me who I am and believing in me as an integral part of their team; and last but not least, my earliest and probably most influential "replacement father" and the most powerful male role model that I have ever had the pleasure of being around (while most people did not realize) – 1980 "Miracle on Ice" hockey team and former NY Rangers coach, **Herb Brooks** for allowing me to see from his perspective and for sharing more training and personnel/general management knowledge with me in short blurbs, than anyone else I have yet to meet.

Introduction

Before we can continue, I feel as if I need to address two important and recurring facets related to being a "god". Leadership and pride. Everyone needs to be led, therefore everyone needs a leader. Henceforth, everyone seeks for their "god". Good or bad, we all have people in our lives who bear influence upon the decisions which craft our reality. At times, we may all seek the advice and direction of others. Whether influence is solicited or not, other people in our lives as well as our environment itself can persistently influence our patterns, habits and decisions, and thusly; impact our circumstances. As we all possess an inherent desire to be led, leaders possess the need-to-lead. When attaining leadership roles, leaders should remain cognizant of the fact that leading is not spoon-feeding. While the latter may serve a necessary purpose for a time, it will become counterproductive and enable negative reliance, while completely undermining the development of skills necessary for autonomy. One of our greatest "god" obligations is that of equipping others to become ethical, reliable and independently functioning problem solvers. Of course, leaders will always have to provide some degree of direction, yet clear boundaries are required in order to avoid personal regression and promote the overall developmental process.

Pride as it pertains to my opinions can be viewed in two ways: the positive type of pride and the negative type of pride. Oftentimes pride can "flip-flop" the median and become confused in its role in leadership. The positive type of pride is a picture of someone who is open to input, is meticulous, detail oriented, and takes great satisfaction in their endeavors; one who wishes to accomplish a goal for the greater good, while building a team, family or organization for the better. This type of pride takes joy in completing a work that affects themselves and others in promoting positive progress or change, yet requires little praise. The negative type of pride encompasses one who remains isolated and shuts others out from providing input. Negative pride can be driven by spite and becomes reckless in seeking a means to an end at any cost. This negative pride is more concerned with quantity rather than quality, is driven by selfish motives, and drives recklessly down the quickest route to the destination, regardless of what important factors are left unaddressed or who gets hurt in the process. This type of pride urgently engages in self- promotion, accepts recognition immediately, and flamboyantly boasts of their accomplishments. So, we need to remember where our pride lies as "gods". You do not want your motives to possess qualities from both the negative and positive facets, as it will become convoluted and may prove to be just as destructive as a pride which operates purely in the negative. With pride, you have to remain on the correct side of the fence or eventually suffer the consequences of no one wanting to interact with you at all. In its purest operational form, positive pride is easily identifiable as a diamond amongst dirt.

CHAPTER 1

Who and Why am I?

Everyone looks up to someone, and often someone looks up to you. We each have our role models, and eventually we serve as role models to others. Dare I say that we may even idolize one or more people? Clearly idolization can be expected from younger folks and normally involves a celebrity of some form. Whether it's an actor or athlete, musician or politician; at times and for some unbeknownst reason, we can look to these figures to provide a template by which to frame our style, impressions, attitudes, and actions. Strangely and rarely will we ever have opportunity to receive actual validation from such a figure. However, if one did have the opportunity to meet such a figure, their inherent degree of essential component powers relative to "validation by emulation" would immediately satisfy the overall influence requirement necessary to effect eventual and almost certain impact. A phenomenon otherwise reserved for a lifetime and series of microcosmic, influential events could potentially be affected within one meeting. I am not a psychologist, yet I do provide intervention on a daily basis in some way, shape, or form. Whether in my own home, community, or career "Dr. Massi" has been on call for decades. Although there may be many factors as to why people become who they are (in the absence of any truly diagnosable condition of course), one's perception of what seems acceptable is based largely upon exposure to certain variables. Balance in media, film, socioeconomic, socio-emotional or plain, old socialization exposure is a prominent contributor to often negative impressions. These negative impressions can often be developed by a variety of "fuels". Equally important to the actual negative impression, is why that impression is received, embraced, and perpetuated. Is it a "phase", a transition of self-realization or a deep-seated emotional conflict? In reality, most diabolical behavior is based in and resultant to some type of emotional conflict. Whether this inner conflict is fed by a stream of negative influence in one's primary surroundings, introduction by prominent visualization, or peppered exposure in transience, one's very own lack of emotional capacity to express, decipher, and/or expel abnormal thoughts is truly at the cortex of whether or not one acts upon these thoughts. Whether an action is slightly askew of normal, or at the complete opposite end of the spectrum, the fact remains that we can influence people to mitigate their behaviors in any setting by providing viable tools through which to lend emotional balance. Application of these tools will always lend to a greater chance of success in one's self, home, family, career, and marriage. Such simple offerings as encouragement, praise, and accountability lend to raising a person's emotional and literal standing, and relative value in the aforementioned arenas of life.

Consider encouragement first; our inherent primary-birth drive is to survive. Get fed and be comfortable. Now think back. Were you always so confident in your abilities to accomplish something? Capable of surmounting challenges that required physical, intellectual, or emotional fortitude? No! You and I were not inherently intent on anything, except for being selfish. Did it take you a while to believe that you could in fact ride a bike or swim? Or did it require some encouragement and sound advice from a trusted influencer? We all NEED encouragement. We need to hear someone else say, "You can do it!" Why? I don't know for sure, yet I believe that based on the fact that we are all "social beings", our imprint for design dictates that we require the encouragement of others. Your confidence or lack thereof, is a direct result of the amount of encouragement you have received in your life. Imagine this, your ability to operate as a human being is a direct result of the influence, positive or negative, that you have received from your primary encouragers.

Directly related to encouragement is praise. It is a by-product of completing a goal. You encourage someone to accomplish a task, and when they do it, you praise or recognize them (or not). Recognition, of course, can also be utilized to address negative behaviors. Yet, in the purest sense, praise normally comes in the face of victory, or as result of achieving a goal. That type of praise is fairly easy to administer. What about praise in the presence of defeat? How one addresses progress amongst defeat is an equally important form of praise. For example, a coach taking the time to dismiss the mistakes temporarily and long enough to capitalize upon the opportunity to recognize progresses made, while lending encouragement towards "perfection". There can and will be plenty of time, normally by design, to revisit and examine the mistakes and how to avoid them. Because the truth is, that at the bookends there is only winning and losing. (even while progress towards a positive goal, lies somewhere in between).

Accountability is within the scope of one's "moral compass" and is greatly influenced by proper or improper administration of both positive and negative encouragement. One's idea of accountability generally becomes either developed or underdeveloped within our own checks-and-balances system.

How would the elements explored in this chapter effect and/or be applied to this example?: "Johnny Z." at 11 years of age emulates his favorite less-than-admirable, yet very wealthy performer "Big lo-lo" and begins to dress and act like him. How he progresses with that emulation will become dependent upon societal feedback. Either his social network will enable this phenomena and progression, or somebody will tell him just how foolish it is, and hopefully he will develop his own identity by referencing his own degree of developed moral compass. There will either be acceptance or suggested termination to the behavior. Thus, the behavior will either cease, wean, or be fed. It is all in the delivery and by whom it is delivered. The average peer or the mailman may not possess enough influence to terminate the behavior. Rather, a figure who is, at that time in life, bigger and more influential than "Big lo-lo" is required. Enter Mom, Dad, brother, sister, etc. to capitalize on the child's inherent need for core-group approval. Now we can expect change. You see, influence like any other "sale" begins at the emotional level. Next on the hook, "The Big Three".

CHAPTER 2

The Big Three

Everyone has a "core" or "primary" life group. This groups' composition by animate creatures forms the idea of core or primary group approval. Approval is expressed through either latent or patent actions by one's inner circle and serves to influence a receiver's behaviors one way or the other. The input offered is critical to the micro-development process of an affected individual. Regardless of how a given core or primary groups' influence may ebb and flow throughout various life stages, I believe there are three distinct categories therein. Although there may be a variety of subdivisions (or sub-categories) to these three main categories, it is an irrevocable truth that each carries an ultimate influence weighting.

For example, we each have *primary lenders* in our lives. They are those representing the highest concentration of daily, direct, and chief influence upon a given person. Within this category of *prima-*

ry lenders, exists the most normally and frequently associated unit - *immediate family*. Excluding extended family, the primary lending component within this category is: parents and siblings of the individual or lack thereof. In instances of the lack of parents and siblings found within the *family unit*, the "stand-in" sub-divsion becomes integral to the developmental process. *Stand-ins* represent people with daily, direct contact and influence upon one another, yet in the absence of being the immediate parents or siblings thereof. In such cases, grandparents, uncles, aunts, or cousins might now play replacement roles by necessity. In either instance, a predominant factor dictating *influence rating* is exposure. Influence rating is essentially the degree of impact (cumulative influence) that a given person will have upon another. Exposure is a key variable to influence, and as a person becomes assimilated to society, it will ultimately result in a turnover of influence to those outside of the household at key developmental turning points and changes in age.

Next, let us recognize the importance of the *secondary lenders* category. This category contains those who we are subject to because of "exposure by mandate". (In other words; non-negotiable subjection.) We WILL see these people while away from our home, and they possess plenty of opportunity to influence, and eventually impact, our development. This represents common exposure to persons against whom we are left with little to no opposition in the matter; which may be inherently problematic. *Lenders* on top of this category are teachers, coaches, and systemic authorities such as principals and deans, as well as daycare personnel. A sub-category within, yet just below the aforementioned lenders includes bus drivers, babysitters, doctors, dentists, clergy, and any other non-optional, yet transient-period contacts. Duration of exposure ultimately drives the level and sphere of influence.

Lastly, we find the *societal* category that represents both the inner and outer periphery of life. This is largely relevant during the post-adolescent, teen and adult phases of life., and will eventually occupy most of a persons' waking hours. Most of the elements within this category are products of our personal choice. The primary lenders here are employers, spouses, children, colleagues, and the idea of government as a whole. These are what seem to be related to the most natural, necessary evolution in a traditional human existence. Secondary elements which may eventually become of lower priority in the progression of life are: Neighbors, friends, network contacts, clubs, and affiliations . In simpler terms; activity outside of traditional developmental progression or recreation are perceived as *luxury*. In reality, the health and balance of our complete existence will eventually become a by-product of our relative commitment to each element within the model. Generally, wherever you place your time and effort dictates the perception of the degree of importance you assign to any particular element.

The aforementioned represents the "primary" or "core" approval groups, but what about the counter-cores that every parent, teacher, coach, or employer might encounter? Guess what, gods? You also have to contend with other "direct" and "indirect" influencers that will lend to a child, student, player, or employee's chemical make-up. The "indirect influencers" in this counter-core are represented by traditional and social media, TV, movies, and a wealth of blog spots, web references, and worldwide transmitted agendas. Receivers begin to assume agendas, perceptions, and opinions vicariously. Recurrent exposure in this category can greatly affect a receiver's perception within a relatively limited amount of time. For example, while surfing the web, a particular story that surfaces in a report just once, might escape the reader's eye.

However, if that story peppers the very landscape of the display and related editorials begin to consume the reader/receiver's sensory faculties, uncharacteristic perceptions may develop, snowball, and eventually gain enough momentum to become an avalanche. Depending upon several factors in the reader/receiver's psycho-emotional make-up, such as past experiences, coupled with current emotional state, the degree to which the information and agendas are processed, received, perpetuated and/or displayed in daily personal actions will differ in potency, whether short or long term. Notoriety and credibility may or may not be affected by the source, yet volume of exposure inherently promotes perceptual credibility. A subtle, yet repetitive "brain-washing" of sorts.

The *direct influencers* in this counter-core are represented by every other Tom, Dick, and Harry who may be encountered on a daily and/or transient basis. As with any other category of lenders, the receiver's emotional status will greatly affect the weight of the influencer's input on any given situation. Generally, this group is composed of people present at the morning coffee stop, gas station, pharmacy, grocery store, or others at our kid's recreational events. Within all of this, we also find our "loop influencers" who technically fall within our own peer category, however, when operating independently, can lend indirect influence to a situation they get looped into. For example, let's say you are both a teacher and coach at your local high school. Parent set A has a problem with your coaching style. They harbor this opinion and remain conflicted at an emotional level, behavioral odds dictates that given the opportunity, they may utilize the next similarly situated authority-type figure to get it off their chest. So, during their younger child's next parent-teacher conference they "inadvertently" express this opinion to another teacher at the same school. In this case, the other teacher becomes the "loop influencer", as they are now drawn into the loop via the subconscious hope of influencing the situation in some way. So, in the absence of all the facts, the unrelated teacher at this conference, attempting to be professional, yet in a quandary, provides some politically correct answers and recommendations. Next thing you know, these particular parents set out to improperly circumvent the correct path for resolution. Subsequently, you now find yourself blindsided with a complicated issue resulting from a conversation with an unrelated, yet important "loop influencer" – your very own peer. You see, while that conversation afforded emotional release and perceived encouragement or maybe even empowerment, it also removed appropriate reason and accountability. This is a difficult concept to fully dissect, convey or embrace within a few sentences. However, it is all closely related to a basic example of the more commonly accepted practice of gossip or "rallying the troops" in hopes of gaining agreement and/or approval of our position in the hopes of influencing eventual resolve in our favor.

CHAPTER 3

Influence

Simply phrased; Influence is the ability to affect another's decisions or actions, while *Impact* is the culmination and sum of the influence we offer. Purely framed; Influence is driven by some motivating factors. For our purposes, I will reflect upon our positions as "gods" and state that, at the end of the day, people generally respond to our influence and guide their compliance drive due to either *fear or respect*. In all instances, position and exposure are decisive and contributing factors. Quick example, let us say you have been living next to an incredibly nice, philanthropic, salt-of-the-earth neighbor named Mr. Jones for the past fifteen years. One day while you and your eight-year-old son are in line at the grocery store, you happen to strike up a conversation with the cashier. You exchange pleasantries, discuss yard work, and mention you and your next-door neighbor share in the responsibilities associated with maintaining a hedgerow between your yards. The cashier inquires as to where you live and for some strange reason, you tell him. He then tells you that he knows exactly where you live and then loudly proceeds to inform you of what a mean idiot Mr. Jones has been to him. Now despite your son having lived next to Mr. Jones all of his life, and despite knowing everything to be opposite of what has just been alleged by the cashier, your son is momentarily influenced to examine the reality of the allegation. So, despite Mr. Jones having bought birthday and Christmas presents for your son every year since his birth, and despite Mr. Jones having stocked him up with a bag full of chocolate just hours ago, your son's perception of the truth is immediately compromised. Why? The inherent influence carried by an adult figure. It does not matter that your son had met the cashier only moments prior. You extended a sort of implied acceptance or consent when you engaged in personal conversation, and further allowed for doubt when you didn't immediately jump to Mr. Jones' defense or refute the allegation. Now, this matter is easily overcome since exposure to this cashier and his unfounded allegation is an isolated and temporary incident. What if we put it in a different context? What if all of the original background about Mr. Jones remained the same. Wonderful friend and neighbor. Philanthropic, year-round bearer of presents. Yet, one day, you, Dad, proclaim within earshot of your son, "I just can't stand that Jones anymore! He is a piece of garbage and I won't even so much as wave to him anymore! He's finished!" Well, now you've just upped the ante! You, Dad ("god") at the top of the primary influencer food chain have just presented a new statement, decree, and "gospel". It doesn't matter that your son knows otherwise, because you are Dad! Despite your son's ability to reason at his current level, this change in perception is powerful and immediate. Poor Mr. Jones doesn't stand a chance, despite having the greatest gifts and largest bags of candy. How impressionable is the receiver (son) in this example? Let's break down the equation purely from the receiver's (son's) standpoint.

Dad is...	Son is...
An adult	A child
Male	Subservient in household
A primary influencer	Subservient in society
An authority figure	Subservient in school

A caregiver	Reliant for care
A provider	Reliant for support
A noted peer influencer	Limited peer influencer, if at all
At the top of the primary influencer food chain	At the bottom of the influencer food chain

Now make the son a daughter instead, and then we have an entirely different set of socio-emotional dynamics that lend insult to injury. What if he's also coach, den leader, club commander, or head of some other extra-curricular activity? What if a scenario meets the duress standards necessary to complete "The Influence Trifecta" that includes three major psycho-influential components present in any one "god". For example; Don is 40 years old and the middle school softball team coach. Therefore, he is an **adult, male, coach** - Trifecta under those circumstances. However, compound the scenario by making him the father of one of the girls on the team, and he would then represent **adult, Dad, male, coach** and suddenly morph into the representation of "The Influence Superfecta".

Well "god's", how important are our words, actions, theories, philosophies and agendas? Who and how will we mold and influence? How innocently impressionable is our receiver audience? Have I ever been guilty of being less than all that I can be? Where do you think I got the material for this book?

In any event, another contributing factor besides admiration for the influencer is the notion of loyalty. You see, as we build relationships, it is truly a two-way street. Like dancing, normally and in most instances, someone takes the lead or "wears the pants" in every relationship. Additionally, that person will also have more to initially contribute or offer to the relationship. A parent, employer, or coach has implicit authority and otherwise commands respect by virtue of their position. Initially, the influencer is the one constantly providing guidance, discipline, correction, admonition, and reward. The receiver is highly moldable and impressionable to the words and actions of the influencer. With every relationship, time proves mutual care and respect for each other, as persons drop their guard and allow for more trust and exchange. Lines of communication open up and inevitably the receiver will be afforded with the opportunity to question and explore previously unquestioned and accepted directives. The respect and trust the influencer begins to develop for the receiver then allows an opportunity to request explanation (not necessarily challenge) given directives, while the receiver feels secure enough in their admiration and respect for the primary influencer to address these concerns. Ultimately, there is a fine line between having a primary influencer expound upon reasoning for directives as part of the education process, and the receiver questioning the authority of the influencer. Additionally, as time transpires, the primary influencer will begin to recognize the contribution made by the other person and both become reliant, yet not codependent, upon each other to feed the relationship as well as any other decisions that may influence effective relational operations. Give and take is a key denominator in any of these relationships. The strength of these relationships will at some point be challenged in the presence of a "better deal" or a "once-in-a-lifetime opportunity." Then the paradox of loyalty is truly put to the test. Employees' loyalties are tested in the presence of better compensation, players tested through opportunities to showcase their talents, and children will be tested to defy their parents in the presence of temptations.

CHAPTER 4

Process vs. Product

So why do people turn out the way they are? Whose fault is it, good or bad? Which "god" dropped the ball? What degree of accountability should the parents, school or society assume? Questions for the ages. Although each case will differ, I am confident in saying "gods" are responsible for the process, but not necessarily the product. In entering these highly tumultuous waters, we must remember that it is only effective to examine this topic with an attitude of shared responsibility. The "gods" here have to own their mistakes and realize their contribution, or lack thereof, to the receiver's eventual chemical makeup. Sure there are instances where despite every stellar effort a person ends up being less than sterling. Might I remind you that God still loves them and would have them turn their heart back to Him, rather than rotting in a jail cell and eventually decompensating into less than a shell of what they could have been. The outcome of a person is largely a "matter of the heart" and how one determines to respond to disadvantages. In other words, undesirable subconscious behaviors require conscious decisions to terminate. Behaviors driven by fear, anger, disappointment, and deprecation require one's commitment to look in the mirror and say, "This is not me, and despite my situations, I can do better than this!" Only then, upon making that declaration and taking ownership, can one progress to a better position for themselves, their family, and society. It is the "god's" responsibility to lend encouragement in a timely transformation for good, as opposed to someone wasting half or more of their life away in a desperate existence. (Faith = Hope = Perseverance) It could be at least loosely argued that we are not victims of our circumstances, but rather victims of our own decisions. Decisions eventually turn into action or inaction, and every action or inaction is driven by a decision which began as a thought. Everyone may intend to make change, but it is imperative to transform intention to action. Perhaps one of our most ultimate obligations as a "god" is to assist in equipping others to thoroughly audit their thoughts before decision converts to action or inaction. This process will ultimately affect their circumstances accordingly. (Might I suggest the reading of one of the most powerful books of all time entitled "As a Man Thinketh" by James Allen.)

Let's take a look at the unfortunately common practice of divorce in our society and the way it can compromise both life's processes, and products. Divorce, while complicated, seems to be the world's "challenged marriage escape clause." I'm not saying that there aren't circumstances which justify divorce; but it is my opinion that divorce in many instances and on many levels is merely an act of selfishness driven by a person's desire for something new and exciting or a result of growing tired of the marriage itself. I find that people create a record of offenses, tally up hurts and disappointments, then later use them to justify their eventual, physical departure (they had emotionally departed long before). They find it easier to walk away as they do not possess the emotional capacity to fix what they already have. Take a look at most divorce situations and the patterns therein. People get out of one broken thing and move along to another, which eventually yields the same result. If a person cannot fix the marriage they are already in, what makes them think that they will fix the next one when the going gets tough or the "lovin' gets old"? Are they not just "trading up to a newer model" that will eventually rust, if not given the proper care and attention required? I could have dedicated an entire chapter to divorce because it is present in varying concentrations across all cultural and societal bounds. Let's take an ideal circumstance where a man and a woman fall in love. They court, do the big engagement and wedding thing, buy the beautiful house, have the best jobs, etc. Life goes on and everything is great, yet, it is time for a divorce. No abuse, abandonment, neglect, anything. It just grows old. Isn't that what you're supposed to do with your spouse? Grow old together? What contributes to this mindset, what part of their process was tainted? Usually, that is exactly the case. Perhaps somewhere, either by exposure, selfishness or desensitization, the underlying thought of the escape clause was lying dormant, began to germinate, and eventually blossomed into a decision, an action, and then a circumstance. When you pair that with society's unabated advertisement of acceptance; this becomes a dangerous cascade of false justification. Was there a divorce in their childhood? Threat of divorce? Did mom and dad always argue or not communicate at all? The unfortunately incredible thing about divorce is that it seems that whether it occurs while a child is ten or thirty, the impact engrains and imprints emotional compromise and deep-seated feelings of relational conflict for the rest of one's life.

Can we as "gods" get to a point where we become so selfish in whatever our endeavor that we simply abandon our responsibility to continually and positively influence because we go into our very own and temporary emotional override? Do we then expect to be afforded with the luxury of arbitrarily reassuming our influence when we feel self-righteousness over those around us? Our actions not only compromise our circle of influence, but ourselves. Now we have a typical best case "process" scenario; Mom and Dad in the home, wonderful health, great finances afforded with all opportunities, peer popularity, wanting for nothing. Why would someone turn out less than perfect under these circumstances? What counter-message was being sent, if any? What does a "god" have to do for their children, players, or employees to turn out great? What is the magic formula? The "gods" are responsible to put the receiver in the best possible positions of advantage, provide emotional support, and encouragement, foster open lines of communication, and avoid emotionally administered criticism. Instead, each "god" should strive to lead, teach, and develop as part of a "global equipping process" which fosters independence, and the eventual evolution of another productive "god" within our society. Short of that, the only real answer is that we remain genuinely vested in and responsible for the process and hope that the product turns out somewhere near how we imagine. Remaining sensitive to the obvious warnings that something is going awry is key to providing timely intervention in the process. Recognizing the warning signs and addressing them immediately, as opposed to ignoring them, creates an entirely different conversation. Do yourself a favor "god"; define what you believe are your responsibilities to the process.

CHAPTER 5

Harness & Project

That which makes us succeed can also lead to failure. We as "gods" must realize certain qualities which make us effective leaders require immense balance and control, otherwise these qualities cause us to come across as arrogant taskmasters. Remember, your determination, drive, commitment, dedication, discipline, and the like may not exactly be commensurate to that of your receivers. Thusly, we as "gods" can suffer and harbor an inherent degree of resentment in attempting to process how someone could not possess or understand our set of ideals. How could those we lead not get us? I mean, don't they know how hard we've worked? Or how accomplished and intelligent we are? Do they know how much we know? People do not care how much you know until they know how much you care. Attempting to lead others to embrace a set of ideals, a mission, a project commitment, etc., can be a very frustrating undertaking. Vision casting even by the most prolific visionaries can be derailed by counterproductive "inner courts" that are unable to embrace the vision. Therefore, a visionary devoid of luminaries by which to light their path is essentially devoid of vision. Herein lays the truth of making sure that you surround yourself with a good "inner court" while equipping others to operate in a degree of proficiency similar to your own. In any case, chalk it up to questions of intellect, emotional capacity, disinterest or sheer laziness; not everyone is going to be us! Whatever our opinions concerning the most effective ways to sell a vision from concept to completion, one factor transcends all opinions; it's all in the delivery.

Quick example– a boss, parent or coach (a lender) assigns a receiver a task. The receiver is physically, emotionally, and intellectually capable of the task, yet falls short in the execution. Out of sheer passion, the lender's response might be, "Are you kidding me? What is wrong with you? Do it again and get it right!" Pretty poor delivery by the "god," no? Now despite the motivation for falling short on the task, let's take a look at this poor response and find shared responsibility. Remember, we already stated that the receiver was fully capable of complying. If dissected, this response consists of two questions and a demand. How should a receiver (subordinate) respond to this lender (authority figure)? "Yes, I am kidding you. I wanted to tease you and fall short of your expectations to elicit your expression of how much of a letdown I am." As for the second question, although the lender may be attempting to express how they expected more from the receiver, what the receiver actually heard was, "You're a joke and a disappointment that I've wasted time on. You are full of shortcomings that I'm hoping you will confess to me." Lastly, as to the demand portion of the response, the message sent here is, "Regardless of how you might feel and the time you may require to recover from the words I've just cut you with, do it again, do it now, and don't mess up or else." Your passion, your drive, your desire for perfection has made you appear to be insensitive, unwilling or incapable of effectively communicating, and a poor leader.

Let's re-examine this situation from the ground up and see how it could have gone completely different. Assume that before you assign the task, you voice your belief in the receiver's abilities and communicate what is expected from them. Despite that prelude and for some deep (or not so deep) and isolated reason, they fell completely short of the expected precision and results required for completion of the task. Your response and delivery here is vital to the continued success of the relationship and any future missions. In short, a better response might be, "I am normally satisfied with every task you complete around here. Unfortunately, I was surprised to find that this didn't go the way I expected. What do you think about the way this turned out?" Now assuming that your subordinate is being completely honest as to what went wrong and acknowledging the shortcoming, you could proceed with a very positive challenge. Something like, "Look, I know that you have the skillset, that's not in question. I mean you could do this in your sleep. What I would like you to please correct is X, Y, and Z so we can mark this as a job well done. I have so much faith in your abilities that I trust you to remedy this thing so I can put your talents to work on the next task." So despite a failed first attempt by the receiver, this lender's response is far better on all fronts. Let us take a closer look at this newly framed response. First, the lender acknowledges the receiver's abilities, thus extending a degree of equality. Further, he exclaims his belief with two short statements that reassert the first statement leaving no question that he acknowledges the receiver's value. Secondly, the lender politely clarifies and provides a directive as to what needs to be corrected. Within this, the lender also expresses a second chance and forgiveness, offering that once corrected, it WILL be marked "as a job well done." Lastly, the lender conveys a noted degree of confidence in the receiver and thus provides a declaration of team security to put him to work on future endeavors. So many positive messages have been delivered in this lender's response (on psycho-emotional and professional levels) while accomplishing the objective of directing remedy and goal. Faith in the receiver, acknowledgment of skills, consecration as a valued team member and a hope for the future. Besides, there is transparent forgiveness. That's a message with a purpose that will translate to the receiver the aspiration to please the lender and challenge themselves to generally be better, and operate with greater effectiveness.

Let's look at three characteristics that could be improperly perceived; *Passion, Motivation,* and *Perfection*. **Passion could easily be construed as anger** and insensitivity when one's unbridled emotions and convictions suddenly manifest as verbal, physical, and facial expressions. *Example:* After winning the State football championship 37 - 0, the winning coach convened his team in the end zone. During his emotional speech, he screamed, "That's why I tell you we will always roll over an inferior opponent as long as we keep our minds right and take them down one at a time." Perhaps everything he stated is correct and true, yet the losing team, as well as some of his team parents, perceived his passion as being insensitive and inappropriate.

Motivation could be construed as obsessiveness in light of being driven by past experiences, good or bad, and aspiring to direct others to succeed. We wish to have others share in the emotions of success as opposed to those of failure. Having made a conscious choice to fully dedicate themselves to a particular goal or mission serves as the fuel in this comparison. This sense of drive, no matter how positive, can be misconstrued and perceived as absolute obsessiveness. *Example:* One Friday afternoon, a CEO convenes the company for assembly in the lecture hall. He states, "Our company continues to raise its stock and corner our market. We stand on the horizon of complete and lucrative control as we near the completion of this project. So in the interests of bettering our future, we will all be required to report on Monday for the completion of the project despite it being a holiday. I'm sure you can all

appreciate my excitement and eager anticipation."
I don't know? Could you? Would you? I mean, if everything he had just reported is completely accu-
rate, then what's one day for job security, company
growth, and a better future? Nothing! (At least in a
narrowly framed opinion) Demanding the surren-
der of a pre-planned holiday may just seem obses-
sive to some.

Perfection could be perceived as narcissism as
it normally pits one's development against an un-
realistic standard. Although there are differing
degrees of perfectionism, the inherent characteristics are rarely viewed as positive or productive,
as the perfectionist's perceptions and expectations
are difficult to convey to or be embraced by others.
Demanding excellence and demanding perfection
are two entirely different animals. Perfection is
normally the perfectionists' perceived idea of excellence that will most probably never be attained by
anyone, not even themselves. A perfectionists' motivation is often destructive, allows no margin for
error, and can stifle the growth and learning processes. You can normally recognize perfectionists
by their loneliness and lack of viable relationships.
Despite the similarities to complete narcissism, the
perfectionist maintains a generally healthy concern

for others, he just doesn't think they can accomplish what they can. After all, "If you want something done right you have to do it yourself. *Example:* Mr. Tompkins has been cutting his grass for 35 years. He knows just how he likes it and takes great pride and appreciation in his lawn. As he is getting on in years, he realizes that he requires some assistance with the maintenance. After thoroughly interviewing landscaping candidates to take over the duties and providing them with detailed schematics on how to conduct the lawn-cutting process, he is certain that he has removed all margin for error, however, the new landscaping guy is not him. He takes great care the first time as he sets out to cut, trim, and blow immaculately and spends nearly twice the time normally allotted for such a job. He is diligent, as well as pleasant and respectful to Mr. Tompkins and leaves the property looking professionally groomed, at least to eyes like yours and mine, but has not quite developed the eye that Mr. Tompkins has for his lawn. So once the landscaper clears the block, Mr. Tompkins gets his equipment out to give the property a once-over and bring it up to his liking. In the process, he manages a pretty good cut on his foot that sidelines him for almost a month. Does he fire the landscaper or begrudge him for getting injured as a result of his having to bring it up to par? Mr. Tompkins just quietly acknowledges that not everyone is him and it will never be good enough – he'll just have to clean it up each time when the landscaper leaves. You see, he recognizes that there is a task to be completed that he can't necessarily complete all on his own and accepts the fact that the only way for it ever to be perfect is to do as much as he can himself. A narcissist bearing perfectionist tendencies on the other hand merely berates the landscaper, fires him then goes on to fire a series of landscapers after that. (In some instances, the high spectrum narcissist doesn't berate at all, rather gains trust and provides an excuse for no longer requiring the services. – but that's for another day.) You see, it's okay to demand excellence from both yourself and others recognizing that it merely means providing the best and most diligent efforts to the task – bringing out your best. However, a level of perfection (usually unreasonable) otherwise taints the process. So really, although unreasonable, Mr. Tompkins is a perfectionist as opposed to a narcissist. Which, of course, proves to possess its own inherent, and destructive tendencies, making neither a truly desirable behavioral type.

In short, factoring in various personality types and perceptions vs. actualities, one needs to remain highly cognizant of how they present and how their presentations are perceived by their audiences. This includes remaining persistently open to the input and constructive criticism of your inner courts, otherwise, you can quickly lose your effectiveness, credibility, and influence as a "god" amongst a majority of your receivers.

CHAPTER 6

Assimiliation

In any organization, whether it is a family, sports team, or business associates, individual differences will be present. In general, we find two extremes with very few falling in between; Individualists and Team Players. You can attempt to develop one's ability or tendency to veer towards either end of the spectrum under certain circumstances, yet ultimately the inherent individual difference will prevail. Recognizing the reality of one's propensity to organizationally assimilate to their given capacity is a key component of success. Recognizing, then choosing to understand the differences, as opposed to the root of these differences, and nurturing the dominant features towards functionality, assists in correctly utilizing individuals in any organization.

Individualists are generally creatures of habit. They normally require little attention or external motivation and largely rely on their own sense of morality, intellect, expectation, and reasoning to drive their management, production, and solution skills. They flourish in situations of isolation and can produce high volumes in their designation whether it be work around the house, on the field, or in the office. Individualists possess a tendency to self-regulate when they fail, as opposed to causing discord. They can be highly functional multi-taskers, and very rarely ask for assistance in the face of being overwhelmed. They fade into silent obscurity in team environments, yet make consistent and notable accomplishments therein.

Team players are social creatures who thrive in multi-dimensional settings. They flourish in team environments, embrace group project stressors, and are driven by a sense of collaborative accomplishment. Team players rely on the motivation provided by a leader and feed off of the entire team from project conception to debriefing. They look to their peers for acknowledgment and acceptance, yet everything becomes a subconscious competition. Often, teamers seek the leader's approval above all else and can fall prey to efforts of self-promotion. They possess the propensity to utilize the team environment as an arena to stand out and seek favor, or potentially promote their own agendas. Type A personalities generally abound in this type and require highly skilled and relevant managers to maintain traffic control and focus. However, when properly aligned, managed and appropriated, these team players can be a highly valuable mission asset within any organization. Within both extremes (Individualists and Team Players); mutiny, discord, and division may only become a risk when there is perceived offense, normally associated with diminishing one's contribution to the overall mission. This may not necessarily indicate a failure in leadership, rather perhaps the existence of underlying rogue, and dysfunctional overachieving. With both bringing a degree of risk, neither may prove to be more valuable than the other, just more so situationally mission relevant. That of course is where tactful assignment, placement, and delegation becomes critical.

So how does a "god" embrace, develop, and delegate to these different function types? Firstly, question how we can nurture the dominant personality traits of a given type to serve an organization's good while infusing some complementary features from one another. I believe the key is balance. In general, you cannot change people, yet you can attempt to elicit "influence-by-exposure" in the personnel resource pool. Aligning different function types with each other in controlled projects and collaborations allows for each to be exposed to different approaches to completing tasks. Assuming that these types are active learners and perceptive enough to recognize, extract, and compare their respective elements, this often leads to the extraction of positive qualities that one can apply in their related function. For example, imagine that the highly functioning individualist suddenly develops through exposure or osmosis, the previously non-existent ability to accurately convey their otherwise concealed thought process and methods utilized to formulate their superior ability to structure and complete tasks. Odds are, the competitive spirit found in a Team player will influence positive qualities within the Individualist without compromising their good function traits. Maybe the Team player will now appreciate the concept of allotting time to independently self-check the relevance of project concepts prior and apart from the team, as opposed to always presenting the kitchen sink in project meetings. This form of self-filtering will almost always result in more efficient team meetings that yield better quality and more cost-effective ideas. Hence, streamlining the processes normally associated with the Team players operations, without otherwise compromising their functional ability. Likewise in this balanced exposure of personnel, perhaps the Team player will influence the Individualist to develop a better sense of collaboration. This is likely to persuade the Individualist to seek peer input in cases of a self-imposed impasse. This will lend to a greater degree of objectivity when considering certain concepts offered by collaborative parties and thusly assist in the determination of what ideas should be developed and pursued. In general, and what we seek to develop here is to assist the Individualist to realize that they can rely on the input of others to remain effective and avoid becoming overwhelmed and otherwise burnt out. The essence of both examples is that the function types gain the tools of clarity and objectiveness to assist in their operations. The long-term benefit to both function types personally and organizationally is invaluable: once again, only if positioned correctly.

The key here is balanced exposure. How do you balance the cross-pollination of each type's characteristics and elements without detracting from the value of dominant traits? As a "god" you have to remain highly active and intuitive in this organizational development method. In any case (family, team, or business) certain variables need to be considered when devising a plan for the personnel development methods to be utilized in the process. One key item to consider is time. The time within the organizations' schedule to accommodate such an effort, as well as the length of time to affect desired results without causing personnel disruption. Additionally, a key feature that cannot be overlooked is the associated personality types within an organization. Different from function types, prominent personality types must be considered when implementing these intervention strategies. We must consider by what methods and to what extent personality types like thinkers, feelers, introverts, extroverts, etc. can be exposed to each other before it becomes counterproductive or even worse, leads to the need for conflict resolution. Look, this is a reality! Whenever you deal with the resource of people, you have to consider emotion. Things like socio-economic differences may also come into play in certain organizational settings. Desensitizing your resources and promoting a better understanding of each other should remain a consistent goal. One major goal to keep at the forefront during these processes is to promote an appreciation for the roles that others play within the organization in hopes that each will come to respect the contributions of their colleagues, team, or family members. Additionally, we aim to reveal what each person possesses as strong suits that can be offered to others in both individual and collaborative capacities. Proactive plan objectives should be previously determined and prioritized as it relates to the process. Utilization of a quantitative scale can also be utilized to track the success and timeliness of the interventional strategies.

CHAPTER 7

Realization

Interest is the essence of impact. Taking a personal interest in someone is a major requirement to influence and the eventual impact thereof. Contributing to the betterment of someone else is truly the embodiment of selflessness. It normally requires a degree of self-sacrifice and self-control. It is usually easier and more economical to reveal someone's faults, however, there is a divine contribution made through patience and leading one to a place of self-realization. Ultimately, we become better people when we can assist in making others better. The reward is often intangible, yet, none-the-less, a reward. Perhaps not immediately evident yet, paying immense future dividends to the overall global process of betterment within one's household, business, community, or team. In the end, the process of self-realization is incredibly liberating for all parties involved.

Now don't misunderstand me. As I had previously stated, it is far easier to simply point out flaws and hope that they are somehow miraculously remedied. However, I assure you that you do have a responsibility to the correction process. Therefore, it is a better option to ensure a productive mitigation process by leading others to realize and acknowledge the issues which lend to their personal development. Although it is quite an involved process, I can assure you that all parties involved will acquire skills that complement all future processes. Inevitably we must choose to understand people, attempt to gain insight into their situation, and develop a mitigation process that will be sound under the particular circumstance.

I interact with personnel and business professionals on various levels daily. In conferring with management, I always preach a message of retention as it promotes healthier employees, companies, and people. In a fast-paced world, employers are faced with personnel alignment decisions almost daily. At first glance it may seem highly logical for an employer to replace someone who is underperforming, however, I lead with this caution; cyclic replacement of personnel can be highly destructive to an organization. Do not read me wrong, there can be a lot of contributing factors that might warrant an immediate replacement of personnel, and depending upon the position and the related infractions, some severances are no-brainers. However, in instances of personnel merely having performance struggles related to a transient life issue, I say remediate. If you have someone who is currently under-performing, yet genuinely does not steal time or money and is not venomous to your organization's mission – make every effort to keep them. Sometimes it is better to influence a known commodity for the good, as opposed to entering unknown territory. Because your other option of course, is to undertake a replacement and hiring process that will take at least a few weeks to yield a viable candidate pool. Out of that small pool, there will be questionables. Further, once you gamble on the decision and make a placement, you can bank on at least a month for someone to gain a base understanding, let alone mastery, of their position. Understanding and efficiency are two distinctly different animals. Afterward, you can only hope that they don't decide that the position isn't exactly what they expected, or not what they want to do. Then you have an entirely different, yet previously encountered set of circumstances. Shortly thereafter, you will find yourself engaged in the same cycle once again.

Let's not forget to mention that there are the termination and unemployment situations to navigate with each employee severance. Additionally, we cannot discount the emotional transitions that occur for remaining personnel relating to both the departure of the previous employee as well as the assimilation and acceptance of the new employee. Set your sights on correcting the correctable and, train, empower, and enable your management teams to face these issues proactively.

In all things, attempting to affect change is very difficult. **You** can't suddenly change people. They have to make a realization about their attitude and its effect, as well as recognize certain latent and unresolved factors they carry with them. Mitigation strategies for promoting realization can be risky. In family, they can cause broad and often protracted chasms to develop. I say develop, because that is what these types of chasms do –not just merely exist, but continue to develop. It seems oxymoronic, but in attempting otherwise positive mitigation, a whole new negative may result. Sometimes in a family, it is better to allow some room for self-realization, when not destructive, and capitalize on an opportunity to lead one through self-examination, as confession and accountability regarding one's actions begin to unfold. Then again, there is inherently more tolerance within the family. However, in situations of staffing whether in business, teams, or other organizations, time is of the essence. Here are a few simple tools to utilize in the mitigation decision-making process:

1) Are you able to "quarantine" the person and their effect?
2) Is it possible to continue forward with reasonably productive operations under the quarantine?
3) Will this quarantine cause major losses to personnel or capital?
4) Is there trust between the mitigating party and the quarantine that will allow for the mitigation process?
5) Can you perform the mitigation while maintaining confidentiality and involving very few, unrelated hierarchy?

Look, let's call this what it is; an intervention! In general, a negative response to any one of the aforementioned questions will make the process that much more difficult. You, as "god" also have to realize that this intervention is going to cost you something. Time, money, minor emotional trauma, frustration, etc. and in general, more of your own personal development in learning to control your thought-to-mouth gate. Attempting to be divisive about the situation will be catastrophic. Transparency with all parties concerned is of the utmost importance as it will establish a genuine trust in the process. In approaching the process you simply have to reveal the facts. Let the person know that you have noticed an evident degree of resentment, unhappiness or declining performance and are having the conversation because you care about retaining them, not necessarily enabling their oppressive nirvana. Expect one, or any combination of spectrum responses from relief, emotional outbursts, anger, fear, defensiveness, flippancy, appreciation, remorse, and of course – denial. Process the responses with a grain of salt and allow for some dead-air as the other person utilizes time to elaborate on their initial response.

Additionally, I assert that when all else fails; *Pray for change*. The testing of your faith should not be reserved for the time when every measure has been exhausted – rather seek divine guidance from the start. Believe me when I say that much like one with a substance abuse issue, any person not prepared to enter into confession and self-examination will be an immovable and impenetrable obstacle until such a time that they are liberated from their arrogance and ignorance.

CHAPTER 8

Chasm, Impasse, Stalemate, & Stand-off

Far too complicated to adequately address in just one chapter, chasm, impasse, stalemate, and stand-off require an entire book to appropriately dissect. The terms are interrelated, yet unique in both frame and scope. As with any of the other terms addressed in this book, the decided variable always comes down to the current and related state of emotion. In summary, the phenomena, frames, and related emotional spectra are as follows:

Chasm: A complete and total separation of perceptions with no apparent bridge or means for resolve, normally a result of exhausting all measures or a time of pure ignorance toward a situation that has developed to a degree of festering, animosity, and even absolute contempt. Persons associated have all but vacated resolution as an option and progress has been halted by deep-seated emotional offenses, often with tangible manifestations.

Impasse: A juncture in conflict when associated persons have decided to accept apparent non-resolve. Resolution is not at the forefront of either person's mind as much as existing with the accepted impasse as an unresolved time in life. Unlike chasm, there is an apparent avenue for resolution preserved, yet often not easily evident to the persons involved in the impasse. Progress is usually hampered by a temporary emotional offense that should resolve with time and eventually allow for the realization necessary to find a means for resolve.

Stalemate: A point in the resolution process where associated persons are temporarily hindered from progress based on positional perceptions. Often, outside impartial observers can lend guidance for resolve as stalemate is normally associated with the involved persons being unsure how to proceed, based partially upon concern for outside perception. Unlike impasse, however, there is normally less harnessed personal offense involved in the matter and timely resolve is probable.

Stand-off: Normally steeped in stubbornness, this is a juncture of conflict where associated persons are waiting for the others to make the first move or be the one to extend the olive branch. Resolve in these circumstances is normally only hindered when associated persons are more concerned to find out if the other side of the table actually cares enough to acknowledge the offense or at least appreciate their position. Immediate resolve is normally associated with the apparent compromise of either or both persons.

In addition to the obvious common denominator of emotion, variables interrelated to the above four terms are: time from the offense, time of removal, time-in-conflict, time-in-resolution process, levels of frustration, socio-economic considerations, and associated external input. States of health and physical distance between two persons also greatly contributes to the aforementioned phenomena. Like the adage, "absence makes the heart grow fonder", absence between persons also allows for physiological adjustments to life and therefore timeliness of intervention should be strongly considered. Sometimes we find that persons feel that issues and offenses are far too painful to continually have to dredge up and tread upon. Never-the-less, when purposing to overcome conflict and engage in the resolution process; clear objectives and boundaries need to be established from the onset to get the parties in the room. Even though expounding upon the more uncomfortable parts of the conflict is necessary and eventual, much can be accomplished by safely and systematically leading up to the perceived offenses. Diving right into the heart of the matter rarely proves to be productive and requires a highly skilled counselor, otherwise, it becomes chaotic and equates to throwing a grenade into the room. Regardless, you will find various feelings of limbo and apparent blindness to the obvious in all of the related phenomena, and this will also lend to the frustration level of the mediating party.

CHAPTER 9

Faith Breeds Hope

At age nineteen, I acted upon a tip. I solicited and convinced a large three-letter company to have me speak at a company-wide regional administrative training seminar regarding "Integrity in Business & Full Circle Concepts." After a lengthy telephone conversation with the training coordinator, we arrived at a hefty speaking fee. I did not know what to charge and did not want to price myself out, so I figured I would negotiate based upon participant attendance. He said that there would be at least 300, yet as many as 500 in attendance as it was mandatory training for most. Having quickly done the math I stated that I would extend a price to him of $5.00 per head which left him wiggle room to provide a light lunch for each participant and come in at around a $10.00 cost per participant from his budget. I then boldly added that the reserve fee would be based upon the cited 300, yet he could compensate me for every other latecomer on the

day of the seminar. He agreed. Upon my arrival for
setup that day, the training coordinator came into
the large auditorium, greeted me then asked if Mr.
Massi had arrived yet. I collected myself, reached
out, retrieved his hand and gave him a power shake
as I stated, "Guy Massi here, excited to work with
your team." I thought he was going to faint. Then
he stated, "Guy Massi Jr.?" To which I replied with
a chuckle, "Surely, you must be kidding." "But I
thought you were... I mean you sounded like...quite
frankly I thought you were much, much older," he
stated with a grin of panic as participants began to
filter in. I brushed off his commentary and capital-
ized on the diversion of entering participants and
went about getting my game face on to bring the
thunder. There were 430 participants in attendance
on seminar day, and I experienced a very comfortable rate of compensation for a nineteen-year-old
who had traveled only about 30 minutes north of
home for this payday.

For some reason, I had faith in myself at a time
in my life when no one else did. Both of my parents
had passed on by this time and the rest of my family
was either scattered or in various rifts which left me
as a man on an island. I don't know if it was by divine intervention or by mere necessity, yet I found

faith in myself which provided such surety, I could do anything; even at the last moment. Often it is easier to have faith in someone other than yourself. Everyone requires encouragement to fill one's belief that they can overcome the faith barrier. For some strange reason, we find it easier to have faith in others. You easily have faith in the mechanic to repair your vehicle or faith in a doctor to treat what ails you. However, when it comes to a person having faith in themselves, they often rely on the input of another (their "gods" especially) to bolster their belief in themselves. Only in very rare instances does someone truly strut with an uncompromising faith in themselves every hour of the day. Normally one requires a regular fill of their faith tank to keep them in the game. This is where faith feeds hope.

Hope is the feeling of peaceful and eager anticipation for something good amid otherwise stormy circumstance. For a circumstance to turn out right, despite the seeming adversity, hope is probably one of the best and most powerful "natural highs" nearing that of nirvana. Hope can make one feel almost superhuman and accomplish almost insurmountable tasks well in a disproportionately small amount of time. Hope fed by faith for a desperately needed raise, fuels effective project accomplishment in the workplace. Hope fuels immense dedication, performance and study over an otherwise small period. Hope is the exact opposite of discouragement. Where hope brings out the best in us, discouragement almost always brings out the worst in us. The faith that feeds this hope is the exact opposite of fear. Feelings of elation vs. feelings of desperation. Whereas discouragement is the most powerful tool to break a person down, hope is the most eventful gift that lifts an addict, the abused or the underachiever out from the depths of darkness. Who categorizes underachieving? Well, the "gods" do! It is comparative and subjective to what the primary lending "gods" deem as an achievement. If a high-powered C.E.O. sees his son land a great and honest job in the maintenance service industry as being an underachievement and holds back his approval, this speaks to lack of faith in his son. This lack of faith feeds a lack of hope and, ultimately, the equation equals discouragement. If that same "god" were to provide approval and express faith that their son would have the highest possible success in any particular vocation, the game immediately changes for the better. Faith now provides hope for success in the field, in society, advancement, promotion, and success in the home. Profound faith from the "gods" forms life's trajectory and leaves a legacy of hope. Speak the profound encouragement necessary to elevate your team, home, family, business, and friends to serve as contributory vital members of society. In a nutshell, faith feeds and hope develops the endurance to persevere. Have you created a legacy of hope in these areas?

CHAPTER 10

Shades of Resentment

It has been said that choosing to remain angry at someone long after they've forgotten what they've done is like "drinking poison and waiting for the other person to die." Likewise, I contend that if anger is like "drinking poison", then resentment is the cup in which it's held. Anger can make one go on each day with conscious animosity toward another, while the offender simply goes about their day without thought or care about you. Anger, vengeance, and unforgiveness are all related in some way, yet in its purest form, anger is almost always developed within resentment. The most effective way to dispel anger is to make a conscious effort to forgive and free oneself from the power, control, and oppression another's wrongdoing has caused in your life. This is easier said than done. However, I've seen many a person controlled by anger become obsessed and further controlled by resentment. This phenomenon usually occurs through transforming passive resentment into an active resentment more so unto the spectrum of contempt and animosity, which potentially controls one's thoughts and actions in familial, personal, and professional relationships. Perhaps with argument only as to actual or perceptual placement and escalation within a continuum; Anger, Resentment, Animosity and Contempt are contained within the same destructive category. For the purposes of this book, let's examine this category from the perspective of what can be called active and passive resentment.

Passive resentment remains very closely related to latent or undisclosed anger. Latent anger is normally associated with an otherwise minor offense or series of minor offenses. Normally, one's thoughts are not consumed in the presence of passive resentment, rather only certain circumstances raise these emotions. For example, the related offender may only be brought to the forefront of your mind if you were to learn of their good fortune, promotion, purchase of a new vehicle, or some other beneficial event. In response, one would experience a compilation of emotions similar to jealousy, envy, and anger that quickly sum up to that of resentment. Accordingly, thoughts and justifications develop as to why the offender should not be entitled to the good fortune because of what they have done to you. They are undeserving and everyone should be made to understand that, yet you may not necessarily stand on a soap box in order to project your feelings.   Basically, your anger is harbored within the cup of passive resentment.

Active resentment, on the other hand, and strangely enough, can be present in both cases of latent or patent anger. For example, you may or may not have clearly expressed your disagreement and subsequent anger relating to your company's decision to abandon your business philosophy as they approach a new client or project. None-the-less, your "hope" begins to revolve around their failure in an "I told you so attitude." Whether or not the new approach succeeds, you begin to actively resent your leadership team. The very sight of the persons associated with the decision and "offense" makes you angry, ill, and frustrated. No matter whether the offenders are present or out of sight, you dwell upon the offense and harbor the degree of anger and animosity that has developed into active resentment.   You become obsessed with their failure and consumed with analyzing justification for your pain. You possess utter disgust and disdain for the offender and require more to get your mind off of the situation as opposed to bringing your thoughts back to it. The resentment associated with the situation, as opposed to the situation itself, consumes your rest, peace, time, energy, and emotions and eventually leads to an inability to objectively examine any situation associated with the offenders. Worse, it begins to affect how you treat those unrelated to the situation, as everyone begins to take on the role of a possible offender or sympathizer. Active resentment is truly a gateway to the eventual development of full-blown contempt, should the active resentment fester and remain unaddressed. This is where the violent hatred and active opposition associated with animosity begins to morph and surface as held within the vessel of active resentment.

Now, what happens when offenses come from the inner sanctum? What if your greatest hurts and offenses have been experienced within your own household, family, or marriage? This is when latent or patent anger, which has evolved into passive or active resentment, needs to become active forgiveness in order for wholeness and healing to occur. Otherwise, the results will only be partial. Once a decision has been made to honor a covenant, the parties must actively involve themselves in the expression and resolution process.

Resentment is one of the greatest, if not the greatest barrier to progress. Many a product or service hasn't reached the market, family vacations have been foregone, or a play not made it to the field as a result of resentment. Resentment rivals just about any emotion and affects many other frames of human interaction like trust and delegation. Resentment is a highly volatile catalyst for negative aggression and anger that requires a thick lid to cover and greatly impedes one's ability to sympathize, empathize, or effectively relate on any level with an offender. Resentment in any team (family, business, sport or coaching system) drastically impedes synergy or unity in moving toward mutual goals. For example, when resentment is present in any team-type setting, progress is nearly impossible without some sort of separation. Let's assume that you are the supervisor of a team strategy project and would rather not include the offender in the project meetings. You could choose to reveal the writing on the wall or just go with it. After all, you are not harboring resentment as a result of a major event, rather a series of small offenses perpetrated against you.

Minor delays in getting assignments to you, "losing" your e-mails occasionally, "forgetting" that you had spoken about an upcoming schedule change, etc. Offenses which on their own may not warrant termination, yet seem perpetrated with purpose. You've lost all ability to sympathize and relate with the offender and now find that you are content with never desiring to interact with them again. Now you have to lead them and be their "god" in the project arena, include them, their thoughts, their ideas, and their perceptions as considerations, while you can barely muster the patience to look at them or let them speak. That level of resentment is a real issue in moving forward.

So how does one move forward in the presence of resentment? Freeing oneself from resentment is akin to kicking a drug addiction. It is a process which will not happen overnight. It requires both traditional and creative strategies to overcome. It requires a conscious and professed personal realization that there is a problem which needs to be addressed. Unfortunately, freedom from resentment requires absolute vulnerability and a complete and total loss of care for what outsiders may think - public perception. All this because generally speaking, developing resentment is often a collaborative effort, whereas freeing yourself from it is a deeply personal process.

CHAPTER 11

Final Chapter?

Could one choose to influence for totally selfless reasons? Strictly for the betterment of an individual and society as a whole? Challenge another's ability to face adversity and come out on top? Contribute to one's social, moral and ethical development and empower them with the ability to "pay it forward"? Solely to contribute to the greater good and establish a new component to build a better global template? All while expecting nothing in return? Well, I give you a resounding yes! It's quite rewarding also. One must also temper the god-complex when using these ultimate opportunities to enable one to find their way. Don't ever intentionally place people in calculated and detrimental disadvantage, believing that you are teaching them something, rather place surmountable controlled challenges in their path by which there can be discernible benchmarks and victories. It is easy to fall prey to the experimental and "oh well, abort mission" mentality if all goes wrong. But remember, we are influencing peoples' lives in our positions. Remember "we are gods"! It's an awesome responsibility. Believe me, you are more vulnerable in these situations, although you may fail to recognize it.

I had an athlete who played football for me years ago and I could tell that things were less than ideal in his household. Nobody was getting beaten and there was food on the table, but you could see that this young man possessed a lot of anger and resentment. It was obvious that life wasn't what he would like it to be and he was struggling with assuming his rightful place in the household. Regardless, his great potential was evident and football was exactly the springboard required for him to establish some self-worth and a sense of accomplishment. He was a bit undersized at the time, yet quite athletic. His glimmers of brilliance were few and far between, but present. I recall a conversation I reluctantly had with him after practice one day. One of the concerns I had was how to make the emotional content of the conversation stick. How to make him feel and remember it for more than thirty minutes, and how to assure that the message wouldn't disintegrate upon his return home. He had to be able to taste the underlying message for all eternity. I recall the one-sided conversation as such, "It's apparent to me that life is not what you want it to be right now. You probably feel as if you are totally out of control and you don't currently possess the vocabulary to describe your feelings. Now all of that may be true, but here are a few other truths. You can control one thing; your actions. You can control the one thing within your control, and that's you! How you react and when you react. Each decision can affect your whole life's path. Right now you can perform to the best of your ability in football. You don't have to be the best player, just the best that you can be. See, right now, football is your thing! No mom or dad or brothers or sisters on the field with you, just you and your team. Control something within your control and that skill will assist you to perform better in life. Challenge yourself to do the best that you can do in anything, and that will always serve to make you better. Extend respect to those that you find it most difficult to do so, and forgive those that have offended you. Don't drink the poison of resentment that came from them and expect them to die. Has anyone done anything illegal to you or violated you?" He shook his head no. I continued, "Anger, well you seem to have plenty of that! For crying out loud, you're allowed to hit people here, legally!

Harness that energy and play it clean. Dispel some of that fury! Never aim to injure! However, nothing is more beautiful in sports than a good clean hit to an opposing player. Fold him up, then help him up. Hey man, it's football." He smiled, patted my shoulder then left.

Fast forward twenty years in my capacity as an executive manager; I had an employee that was going through an unbearable marital and family situation, and subsequently failing at work. The same concept from the football player was paraphrased like this: "Look, I know life sucks right now. You don't want to get out of bed or do anything. I get it! But you're failing at work. You aren't contributing. You are doing nothing. You have no control over your situation right now. I know. You are, however, in complete control of your job performance. Choose to excel. Choose to accomplish. Choose to improve. It may translate into good for your situation at home. It's up to you! Now I'm not saying that work is more important than family, and I'm sure you are sick in ways you can't quantify, but this is it. You will either rise above, or fire yourself. That, you can control.

Never diminish someone else's problem. Remember that it is a problem or issue to them. It is their issue, their fear, their worry, their burden, their problem at that time. You can attempt to rationalize emotion sometimes, although the feeling is not fact. That doesn't matter. Looking back, I'm sure that we would all say that the problems we faced at various junctures in life weren't problems at all. They may have been events, challenges or circumstances that gave way to opportunity, victory, change, etc. Nevertheless, they seemed like problems at the time. Assist others to see the good, the opportunity to reap something from a challenge which makes them better and empowers them to make others better.

Sometimes you have to be the stand-in moral and personal compass, really be a coach, someone's "god." Sacrifice the time and effort required to lead someone out and away from darkness. Encourage those who may be difficult to encourage. If they choose not to follow, try again, and if they dismiss you, be gently inclined and responsive to their wish. Often, time will provide for the wake-up call and they'll reflect upon the value you offered, maybe even seek you out. Choose to understand others, yet don't enable destructive patterns. Contribute to your development by contributing to that of others. Proceed with caution and a purpose, and always remember that, **we are gods!**

Glossary of Terms

Active Resentment: Can be associated with either latent or patent anger toward an offender that has developed into a deep and active form of resentment that consumes the thoughts and actions of the offended.

Audiences: Those receiving a message or example that impacts their perceptions and/or decision making processes.

Chasm: A complete and total separation of perceptions with no apparent "bridge" or means for resolve, normally a result of exhausting all measures or a time of pure ignorance toward a situation that has developed to a degree of festering animosity and even absolute contempt. Resultant to having exhausted all measures or pure ignorance of a situation to a point of festering in dismissive animosity.

Core or Primary Group: This group is comprised of the family, teachers, and societal classifications unique to a given person.

Direct Influencer: One with the most exposure, opportunity and influential power over another.

Expression and Resolution Process: A process within any "organization" that involves an intentional process by which persons therein agree and are made to become part in a process by which to express sources of resentment to actively resolve disorder with the particular organization.

Family: One's most closely related unit of "primary lenders" by either blood or exposure. Those who normally carry the highest influence ratings.

Function Types: Classifications of personality types within any given setting, i.e. work, home, school. Usually associated with one's ability and method for completing tasks.

God-Complex: Either an obvious or very well secreted mindset, habits and/or behaviors by a person to engage in absolute control of their own life and the manipulation and control over others for "sport", amusement and/or their own narcissistic fulfillment, without care for the effect on others (victims).

Impact Impressionism: A type of exposure that possesses an inordinately high degree of impact vs. exposure time. Normally related to a message, visual or otherwise, delivered by a source with either a permanent or temporary high influence rating, i.e. family, media, or celebrity.

Impasse: A juncture in conflict when associated persons have decided to accept apparent non-resolve.

Indirect Influencer: One with controlled exposure and opportunity to influence another.

Individualists: A true creatures of habit function-type who normally require little attention or external motivation and largely relies on their sense of morality, intellect, expectation, and reasoning to drive their management, production, and solution skills. They flourish in situations of isolation and produce high volumes in their designation whether it means work around the house, on the field, or in the office.

Influence Rating: The degree of impact possessed by a person or classification over another, normally directly correlated by actual societal rating and time of exposure.

Influencer: Someone with the opportunity to impress upon or influence another's actions and/or perceptions. This broad classification includes that of Primary Lenders, Secondary Lenders, etc.

Inner Court (or Inner Circle): The most intimately situated to a person, regardless of their preceding classification. These are the persons we rely most heavily upon and remain most transparent with.

Lender: Someone in a position to influence any given person's actions or perceptions.

Loop Influencer: Someone who happens to be similarly situated in the same operating classification as yourself, who is provided with the opportunity to indirectly influence a situation's outcome in a way that will directly impact your standing.

Non-optional/transient period contacts: A classification comprised chiefly of "Secondary Lenders" or persons such as bus drivers, babysitters, doctors, dentists, clergy, and any other non-optional yet transient-period contacts. Time of exposure ultimately drives the influence rating and categorization.

Offender: Any person within any "organization" who has been identified as having committed an offense toward another, whether actual or perceived.

Organization: A term generically utilized to refer to any unit or body comprised of integrally functioning ancillary parts or members, including that of a business, family or team.

Passive Resentment: Associated with latent, secretly harbored anger against an offender that has developed into a deep, silently held, unexpressed and subconscious level resentment that generally only surfaces in the thoughts of the offended person circumstantially.

Personality Types: Different from function types, personality types are more intimately associated with the surface level emotional representation of a person and normally thought to be represented by reference groups like thinkers, feelers, introverts, extroverts, etc.

Personnel: A term generically utilized to describe the functioning parts within any "organization" such as employees, coaches, siblings, spouses, children, colleagues, etc.

Primary Encourager: A broad term used to describe the spectrum of persons that could bear most significantly onto Receivers. Not necessarily from the classification normally associated with that of Primary or Secondary Lenders, yet bearing primary exposure and influence (normally good) onto that of a Receiver.

Primary Lender: The daily, direct, and chief influencer in any given classification of persons. Normally correlated within the home setting of an individual and comprised of parents, siblings, and family.

Receiver: Any person subject to an Influencer's input.

Secondary Lender: The daily, direct contact classification of influencers that are not immediately present as a parent, sibling, or family member, yet maintain enough significant exposure in a person's life.

Social Network: A classification encompassing all of a Receiver's influencers regardless of relation.

Societal: A classification of primary and secondary lenders that represent and impact decision making processes by either inclusion or exclusion. This may be called an emotional or tangible needs-based classification.

Stalemate: A point in the resolution process where associated persons are temporarily hindered from progress based on positional perceptions.

Stand-off: Normally steeped in stubbornness, this is a juncture of conflict where associated persons are waiting for the others to "make the first move" or be the one to "extend the olive branch."

Teacher: A classification of primary and secondary lenders that represent a regularly mandated exposure role.

Team Players: A highly social yet competitive function-type that thrives in multi-dimensional settings. Team players flourish in team environments, embrace project stressors, and are driven by a sense of collaborative accomplishment. Team players rely on the motivation provided by a leader and feed off of the entire team concept, and also look toward their peers for acknowledgment and acceptance. Often, Team Players attempt to promote personal agendas in their various operating capacities.

Volume of Exposure: The cumulative time of one's exposure to a lender that directly affects the impact of the lender's overall influence upon a receiver. The cumulative time of exposure can relate to high concentrations over short periods, or repeated and sustained exposure over longer and/or transient periods.

About the Author

After having lost their first child, Guy Massi was born to a middle class husband and wife (Everett and Frances Massi) amidst the highly affluent community of Rye, New York. As an overweight child, Guy was shy and only suffered further challenge when his father passed while he was only eleven years old. Guy was driven into employment by the time he was eleven years old working at a local grocery store, and summers with his family of painters. Despite his challenges, Guy remained very active in athletics playing football, baseball and ice hockey, as well as performing in a local band that went on to become regionally popular. In commenting on a pivotal opportunity in his life, Guy states, "The New York Rangers saved my life!" Shortly after the passing of his father, he became a practice assistant with the New York Rangers professional ice hockey team. Not too long after, Guy was introduced to the Rangers' new head coach, Herb Brooks. A man of few words (mostly important ones), Herb began to forge a very private relationship with Guy that influenced many of his life's decisions. Guy recollects that he became enamored with the Russian physical training systems mostly because of Herb's interests, and he learned more energy system conditioning theories from Herb, then probably anyone else. It was the eventual evolution of these interests that lead Guy to begin boxing and martial arts in addition to the other sports, as a means of weight loss and physical development. Additionally, he played short stints of ice hockey within various professional ice hockey leagues. Guy received his first strength and conditioning certification at eighteen years old, and attended SUNY Westchester and SUNY Cortland for undergraduate studies. He continued to develop a career path providing fitness and athletic development coaching to work-force and athlete clientele, while working as an expediter in the aerospace industry, attending massage therapy courses, and serving as a part-time reserve police officer. Around the age of eighteen, Guy was struck by the loss of his mother and the ensuing unfortunate battle by a family member to take his family house and inheritance away from him. Sleeping in his car some nights, Guy was moved by an "entrepreneurial spirit" that fostered his building a very lucrative fitness coaching and organizational development business. Yet, it was at the urging of a close police officer friend that he took the police test in an effort to demonstrate a more easily translatable and apparently more sustainable career path. After being hired by a fairly busy Westchester County, NY municipal department, he entered into another decade of his exposure to law enforcement, while enjoying a highly decorated career in foot, bicycle, and vehicular patrol. He was then promoted to the rank of Sergeant, supervising police personnel some five years after his initial hire. During this time Guy maintained and complimented his strength and conditioning as well as business development knowledge – operating both his fitness/athletic development training, and canine equipment supply businesses as side jobs. A police officer serving during the 9/11 era, he was unfortunately injured in the line-of-duty during a completely unrelated incident. After enduring a bitter battle for both his rights and benefits, he separated from service and segued into a completely civilian life. Jumping into what he already knew best, Guy immersed himself, joined forces with some industry friends, and re-branded his fitness training and athletic performance business to focus on developing everyone from youth to professional athletes, military and emergency service personnel, as well as civilian work-force, and home-force clients. Nowadays he presents both nationally and internationally on the subjects of strength and conditioning, athletic development, safety, mindfulness, and business/personal development – with the ultimate goal of impacting personal and professional growth through sustainable change. His company has developed athletes from practically every sport within the youth, high school, collegiate, Olympic, and professional levels while currently maintaining board seats within industry relevant groups in order to compliment the development and evolution of related industries, and himself. By his own admission, he never feels content with his level of development and perpetually immerses himself in means that are meant to positively affect his own personal growth. One of these means is his persistent obsession to positively impact others by delivering a message intended to deter or arrest a path of destructive personal, financial, career and relationship decisions. This book is truly a parallel chronicle of sorts to his own challenges to discover truly positive role models and encouragers in his life. This book is a personal letter of warning, enlightenment, and hope to the reader.

CPSIA information can be obtained
at www.ICGtesting.com
Printed in the USA
LVHW020712310720
661937LV00009BB/249